CREEPY, KOOKY S

Mysterious Mummies

Ron Knapp

Enslow Publishing
101 W. 23rd Street
Suite 240
New York, NY 10011
USA
enslow.com

Published in 2019 by Enslow Publishing, LLC.
101 W. 23rd Street, Suite 240, New York, NY 10011

Library of Congress Cataloging-in-Publication Data

Names: Knapp, Ron, author.
Title: Mysterious mummies / Ron Knapp.
Description: New York : Enslow Publishing, 2019. | Series: Creepy, kooky science | Includes bibliographical references and index. | Audience: Grade level for this book is 5-8.
Identifiers: LCCN 2018015008| ISBN 9781978504523 (library bound) | ISBN 9781978505537 (paperback)
Subjects: LCSH: Mummies—Juvenile literature.
Classification: LCC GN293 .K64 2019 | DDC 393/.3—dc23
LC record available at https://lccn.loc.gov/2018015008

Printed in the United States of America

To Our Readers: We have done our best to make sure all websites in this book were active and appropriate when we went to press. However, the author and the publisher have no control over and assume no liability for the material available on those websites or on any websites they may link to. Any comments or suggestions can be sent by email to customerservice@enslow.com.

Portions of this book originally appeared in *Mummy Secrets*.

Photo Credits: Cover, p. 1 Andrea Izzotti/Shutterstock.com; p. 5 Insights/Universal Images Group/Getty Images; p. 8 Andrey_Popov/Shutterstock.com; pp. 11, 21 AFP/Getty Images; p. 13 Gianni Giansanti/Gamma-Rapho/Getty Images; p. 16 Robert Harding/Getty Images; p. 18 Jaroslav Moravcik/Shutterstock.com; pp. 26, 37 Heritage Images/Hulton Fine Art Collection/Getty Images; p. 28 Avis De Miranda/Shutterstock.com; p. 29 allou/Shutterstock.com; p. 31 DrimaFilm/Shutterstock.com; p. 32 Christian Kober/AWL Images/Getty Images; p. 34 Chronicle/Alamy Stock Photo; p. 40 RIA Novosti/Science Source.

Contents

Introduction

If left alone, dead bodies don't last. Without blood distributing nutrition and oxygen, they begin falling apart. Bacteria, tiny one-celled organisms, begin breaking down the body. This process is called decomposition. Gases are released as the body decomposes, or rots. Worms, birds, and larger animals may begin to feast on an easy meal. Hundreds of flies lay eggs in the rotting body. Soon it's covered by hungry little maggots, or fly larvae. The skin peels away. Eyeballs disintegrate. Fur turns to dust. After a few months, there is nothing left but bones. And after a few years, they are dust, too.

Today we go to a lot of trouble to stop the decomposition of human bodies. Funeral homes preserve them by removing blood and replacing it with embalming fluid, which contains formaldehyde and other chemicals.

People are now buried in heavy wooden caskets placed inside concrete boxes called burial vaults. Cemeteries are filled with tombstones identifying the dead and marking their burial sites.

The mummy of a Chinchorro baby is displayed at a museum in Chile.

Modern humans are not the first people who have gone to a lot of trouble to honor the bodies of the dead. The Chinchorro people of Chile produced the oldest discovered mummies, or preserved bodies, more than seven thousand years ago. They removed all the internal organs and replaced them with grass or ashes. Masks and wigs covered the head. Finally, the bodies were painted black and buried in the ground.

Scientists think the Chinchorros mummified almost everybody, not just their leaders. So far, more than two hundred of them, adults as well as kids, have been found. The Chinchorros didn't use chemicals. With the internal organs gone, the dry climate quickly dried out the skin. Without moisture, decomposition stopped.

Two thousand years after the Chinchorros, ancient Egyptians began mummifying their dead. Egyptian embalmers knew that moisture speeds decomposition. They dried their dead by first packing them in salt. Mummification was expensive, so only royalty and the rich were mummified.

But not all mummies were produced on purpose. Some of the most interesting ones have been preserved by accident. If a body is frozen immediately after it dies, it can last for thousands of years. Freezing stops decomposition.

The best preserved mummies have been discovered in wet spongy ground called bogs. The acidic decayed plants crowd out the oxygen. Without oxygen, bodies can't rot. Mummies have also been created by volcanoes.

Mummies are cool. They are the stars of some of the scariest horror movies. At museums, everybody wants to see the real mummies. Curators have filled display cases with ancient bodies wrapped in strips of linen.

Mummies are a fascinating window into the past. They give us clues about the lives and cultures of the people who came before us. The condition of the skin and bones reveals whether or not the person had to do tough, physical labor. Sometimes it's possible to examine their final meals by looking into what's left of their stomachs. The hair of the Chinchorro mummies revealed that their children had accidentally been poisoned by arsenic in their drinking water.

From prepared mummies, we learn a lot about their societies. They preserved the bodies so they would be ready for an afterlife. Other beliefs demanded human sacrifices.

The mummies and the other evidence that is left don't answer all our questions. Archaeologists continue to dig. Scientists continue to examine what they find. History comes alive when you look into the face of somebody who's been dead for thousands of years.

CHAPTER 1

Ötzi the Iceman

Ötzi (ET-see) was in trouble. Somebody wanted him dead.

It was spring in the Ötztal Alps between Austria and Italy. As he climbed out of a green valley up a mountain, the trees disappeared and the temperature fell. Ötzi was ready for the cold. He was wearing a deerskin coat and a fur hat. His leggings were made of animal skin. Grass stuffed in his bearskin shoes helped keep his feet warm.

Ötzi was armed with a dagger and a copper-bladed axe. He carried arrowheads, but he hadn't finished carving them. His long bow wasn't strung.

A day or two before, he had been attacked by somebody with a knife. Ötzi had saved himself by blocking the knife with his right hand. He was badly wounded. As he climbed, the hand was a painful bloody mess.

Ötzi lived in the Otztal Alps mountain range.

But Ötzi was not alone. Somebody was closing in. This time there would be no knife fight. His attacker didn't want to get close. Maybe he thought Ötzi was too strong, too dangerous. So he loaded an arrow into his bow. Ötzi probably never saw him.[1]

The stone arrowhead hit him in the back and stuck into his shoulder blade. Ötzi fell into a snowy trench. He was in a mountain pass 6,500 feet (1,981 meters) above the valley. His attacker tried to retrieve his arrow, but it broke.

Soon Ötzi was dead. His body disappeared under the snow and ice. The frigid environment kept him stuck exactly where he was, preserved under a glacier just a few feet above him. Nature had created a frozen mummy!

Ötzi Is Discovered

The Iceman might have remained frozen forever, but in March 1991 there was a violent storm over the Sahara Desert. Dust blew north from Africa to Europe. Some of it settled on his mountain in the Ötztal Alps between Austria and Italy.

The dark dust absorbed much more heat from the sun than the white snow ever had. Soon the top layers of ice were melting. Finally, for the first time in fifty centuries, the sun was shining again on Ötzi the Iceman.

He was found on September 19, 1991, by a pair of German mountain climbers. At first, they thought they were looking at the head and shoulders of a doll sticking out of the ice. But when they got closer, they could see that the Iceman was human.

At first, nobody was concerned about the body found in the ice. It wasn't unusual for skiers and climbers to get lost in the Alps. Frozen bodies were often found whenever the weather warmed and a few inches of the snow melted. The Iceman didn't appear to be anything special.

Soon after the discovery, several hikers climbed up the mountain to have a look at Ötzi. They chopped at the ice with ski poles and axes in an attempt to free the body. While they worked, they broke the frame of his backpack and snapped his bow. Some of them ripped off pieces of his coat for souvenirs. An impatient policeman brought up a jackhammer to finish the job. It blasted away a chunk of the Iceman's hip. It took four days to get him out of the ice.

Not Just Another Skier

Rainer Henn, a forensic expert, was probably the first to suspect that Ötzi was not just another frozen skier. Ötzi's knife had a wooden handle and a blade made out of a piece of flint more than an inch (2.5 centimeters) long. Flint was the rock used by many ancient peoples for arrowheads.[2]

Once the body was free, it was packed in a bag and flown to a nearby Austrian village. There, the left arm was broken when it was stuffed into a coffin for a car ride to Innsbruck. For thousands of years, Ötzi's body had been undamaged, but in four days, the rescuers had almost wrecked it.

Konrad Spindler, an archaeologist in Innsbruck, was shocked when he saw the Iceman. "I needed only one second," he said, "to see that the body was four thousand years old."[3] It was the axe that caught his attention. The 4-inch (10-centimeter) blade appeared to be bronze. Leather thongs soaked in tree sap held it to the handle. Spindler knew bronze tools were used around 2000 BCE.

When the axe was examined more closely, the blade was found to be made of copper. Prehistoric men in Europe had used copper long before they had used bronze. The experts finally decided that Ötzi had lived around 3000 BCE. His was the oldest preserved body ever found.

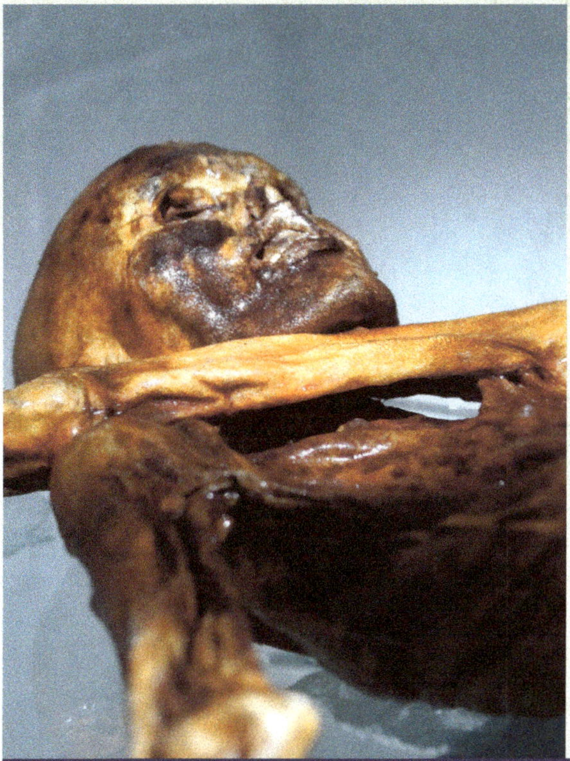

Ötzi's head and upper body are well preserved.

What About His Name?

Ötzi the Iceman left no records. He couldn't write. So how do we know his name? We don't. Ötzi is just a nickname derived from the Ötztal Alps, the mountain range where he was found. Ötztal is a German word since that's the language most people speak in Austria. The two dots above the "O" are a German pronunciation guide called an umlaut.

Why Was Ötzi Murdered?

Experts soon began studying the body of Ötzi the Iceman. They decided that he had been about 5 feet, 3 inches (160 cm) tall and weighed about 110 pounds (50 kilograms). Today Ötzi would be considered a small man, but 5,300 years ago, his size would have been about average.

When he died, he had been about forty-five years old. Most of the men then did not live to be that old. Ötzi's life had not been easy. His teeth were badly worn. His nose and several ribs had been broken and then healed. His hips, shoulders, and knees showed a lot of wear. There was some damage to his skull. He had banged his head or been whacked with a weapon. His lungs were black with soot because of the smoky fires that kept him warm.[4]

Ötzi had dark, medium-length hair. His body had very little fat, so he was a thin man. His stomach still held traces of meat, grain, and plants. The skin on his chest, lower back, wrist, and legs had sixty-one tattoos, all lines and crosses. They had been made by rubbing charcoal on shallow cuts.

At first scientists figured Ötzi had just stopped to rest, then fell asleep and froze to death. But in 2001, they

The Curse of Ötzi?

There's a legend of a curse that befalls those who worked on Ötzi. Seven people involved with the Iceman's discovery had died within a year. What killed them? Heart attack, brain tumor, multiple sclerosis, blood disease, car crash, avalanche, and mountain-climbing accident. But hundreds of people worked on Ötzi's discovery, recovery and examination. After almost three decades, most of them are still alive and well. Scientists think the idea of a curse is ridiculous. Archaeologist Tom Loy was one of the "victims." Before his death, he dismissed the "curse." It was simple, he said. "People die."[5]

found the arrowhead still stuck in his shoulder blade. Today experts are still arguing about the exact cause of death. Some think he bled to death almost immediately after the arrow hit.[6] Others figure he lived long enough to freeze to death.[7]

Scientists recreated how they believed Ötzi looked when he was alive.

But who was Ötzi's killer? We'll probably never know.

Most experts believe Ötzi was an important person in his village. Not everybody would have carried a copper-bladed axe. His striped goatskin shirt, experts believe, was only worn by the upper classes.

Perhaps Ötzi was killed by members of a rival tribe. At first, he was able to fight them off, but his hand was injured and they kept following him. Finally they put the arrow in his back.

But other researchers believe Ötzi might have been killed by somebody he knew, somebody who wanted the murder to be a secret. One of Ötzi's friends or relatives might have recognized the fatal arrow so the killer tried to pull it out. None of Ötzi's fine possessions were taken. Maybe the killer was afraid they would be recognized as evidence against him.

But for fifty centuries, nobody found Ötzi. His tribe never knew what had happened to him.

Today the body of Ötzi the Iceman rests in a refrigerated chamber in a museum in Bolzano, Italy. Scientists continue their work unraveling the mysteries of a man who has been dead for more than five thousand years.

CHAPTER 2

Tutankhamun the Boy King

Akhenaten was dead, and ancient Egypt needed a new pharaoh, or ruler. The new ruler would be his son, Tutankhaten, also known as King Tut.

It was a tough time for the powerful country. Akhenaten had confused and angered his people. For centuries, the Egyptians had worshipped dozens of gods. But Akhenaten said there was only one god: Aten, the god of the sun. He closed the temples of the other gods and put their priests out of work.

Tut probably didn't understand the controversy. He was only nine years old.

Like the other boys of Egypt, his head was shaved except for a long, thin braid that hung down his neck. He wore jeweled ear-rings that dangled down to his shoulders. His eyes were outlined in dark makeup. But unlike most of the other children, Tut had trouble walking. His left foot was twisted and crooked. He needed a cane or a walking stick to get around.[1]

Three thousand years ago, Egypt was the most powerful civilization on the earth. For centuries, the Egyptians had built pyramids, beautiful temples, and monuments along the Nile River in the middle of the desert. The country was ruled by a series of pharaohs.

The Head of Nefertem

Do you want to see what Tut looked like when he was a kid? Check out the little wooden statue now known as the Head of Nefertem. It's less than a foot high. That's the boy king's head poking out of a blue lotus plant. There is no hair, only stubble. Tut's head has been shaved but it's time for another haircut. His ears are pierced for his long, dangly earrings. His eyes are heavy with dark makeup made from soot. This is the only depiction ever found of Tut as a child.

The Head of Nefertem depicts young King Tut's pierced ears and eye makeup.

At Tut's coronation, he was married to Ankhesenpaaten, his half-sister. She was only about twelve years old.

Life was good for royal Egyptian children. The boys wrestled, went swimming, and shot arrows from bows. They rolled dice and moved playing pieces around a board game called senet. Since Tut was in the royal family, he had learned to read and write in the complicated picture language called hieroglyphics. He also could add, subtract, and multiply.

After he became pharaoh, Tut probably had no more time for playing. His days were spent with priests and tutors. When he was still young, the country was ruled by his advisers, but even they had to bow down to the little pharaoh. As Tut got older, he was given more responsibility. Soon he would be running the country on his own. As they became teenagers, Tut and Ankhesenpaaten fell in love and had at least two children.

By then, King Tut had been convinced that Aten was not the only god. The temples of the other gods were reopened and their priests went back to work. The royal couple changed their names to Tutankhamun and Ankhesenamun to honor Amun, once again the king of the gods.

At nineteen, Tut suddenly died, and Ankhesenamun married an old priest named Ay, who became the new pharaoh. Within a few generations, the boy king was almost totally forgotten.

Tutankhamun's gold death mask covered the mummy's head.

Carter Finds the Pharoah

In 1916, a British archaeologist named Howard Carter (1874–1939) came to Egypt looking for what was left of Tutankhamun 3,200 years after the pharaoh's death. Carter knew that the ancient Egyptians had buried their pharaohs in tombs cut out of rocky hills in the desert. They surrounded the bodies with gold and jewels. The tombs were so filled with treasures that they were targets of thieves for thousands of years. After careful study, Carter decided that the tombs of all the pharaohs except Tutankhamun had been looted thousands of years before. He was convinced that Tut was still buried in an undiscovered tomb in the Valley of the Kings. Finally on November 4, 1922, Carter and his crew found a series of steps carved into the rock. Carter's workers emptied the stairway of sand and rocks and realized they had finally found the final resting place of Tutankhamun.

The tomb wasn't just a hole for the body—it was four rooms cut into the side of the hill. The rooms were filled with golden statues, chests, and beautiful vases. There was also a chariot that the king had used and the feathers of a bird he had killed while hunting. On the sides of chests and the back of a golden throne were pictures of Tut and Ankhesenamun. There was also a little chair he had used when he was a boy, as well as a toy lighter and a game of senet.

One of the rooms was filled with a wooden box covered with gold. Inside, Carter found a stone box called a sarcophagus.

When the top was removed, he found a wooden coffin, covered with gold, in the shape of a body. Inside of it was another wooden coffin, just a little smaller, but also covered with gold. Inside that one was the third and final coffin, but it wasn't made of wood. It was built out of solid gold.

Face to Face with King Tut

Inside the third coffin, Carter finally found what he was looking for. There was the pharaoh's body wrapped in yards and yards of linen. Over the top of it was a beautiful gold death mask decorated with hundreds of jewels. Each of his fingers was wrapped in a gold tube. Daggers, rings, bracelets, collars, and jewels were wrapped in the linen that circled his body.

When Carter finished taking off all the linen, he could finally see what was left of Tutankhamun's body. The king had only been about 5 feet, 4 inches (162.5 cm) tall. His ears were pierced, and his head and chin had been carefully shaved. His liver, lungs, stomach, and intestines had been removed, dried in salts, anointed with oils, and wrapped in linen. They were found in tiny coffins in another room of the tomb. His shriveled heart was the only organ left in his body.

Tutankhamun's skin was brittle and discolored, but it was still there. The Egyptians had kept the body from decomposing by storing it for two months in natron, a combination of salt and

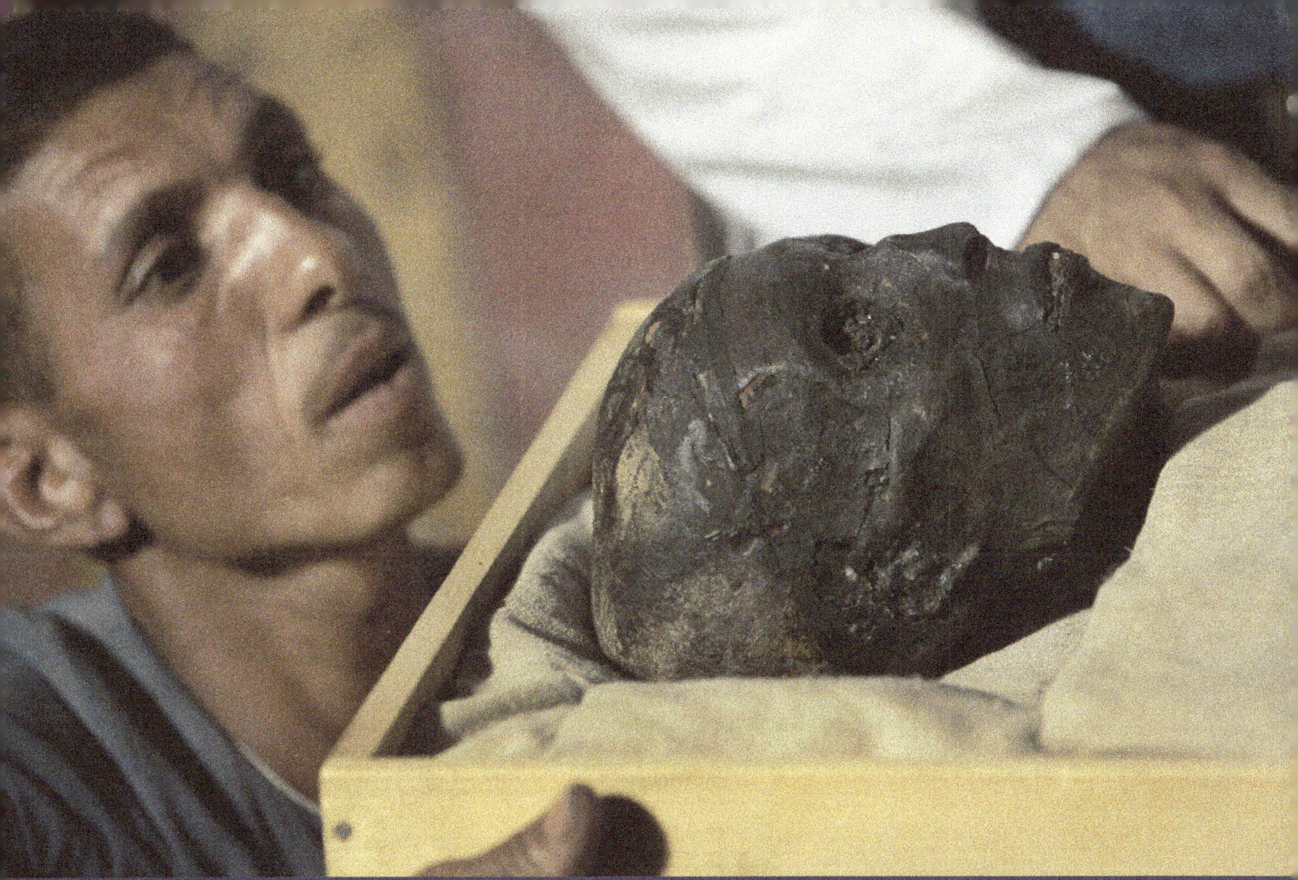

An archaeological worker examines the head of King Tut's mummy.

baking soda that is found naturally in Egypt. This was stuffed inside the body, too. That removed all the moisture before it was wrapped up in linen.

The pharaoh's body was preserved because his people believed he was setting off on a long journey. He would be reborn in the land of the dead. His tomb was filled with his possessions. The rooms were stuffed full of furniture, toys, weapons, and clothes. So he wouldn't be hungry, many baskets of food lined the wall. Because he would need servants in his new life, hundreds of tiny statues called *ushabtis* were scattered throughout the tomb. In the land of the dead, they would come to life and go to work for him.

Was It Murder?

Tut was well prepared for the land of the dead, but how exactly did he die? In the thousands of hieroglyphics found written and carved in the tomb, there is no mention of what happened to him.

Carter found a small scar on the pharoah's cheek. Maybe he had been wounded in battle or hurt in an accident. In 1968, further testing and modern X rays revealed something else. Tut's skull appeared to be damaged, possibly caused by something that had banged into his head. Could he have been murdered? One researcher suggested that Tut was clubbed to death while he slept.[2]

More recently, CT scans revealed damage to his chest. Maybe he was kicked by a horse. Chariots, pulled by horses, were used all over Egypt. Then researchers found considerable damage to the bones on the left side of his torso. Maybe he had been run over by a horse or attacked by a hippopotamus.[3]

In 2013, researchers even "proved" that the damage to his body was caused by a terrible chariot crash.[4]

But today experts believe that most of the damage to Tutankhamun's bones happened after his death. Maybe the embalmers had been too rough with the corpse. Perhaps Carter had damaged the mummy removing it from the coffins.

They are quite sure his twisted left foot made it difficult to walk. There were 130 walking sticks found in the tomb.

But there is one injury that apparently happened before Tut's death. His left femur, or thigh bone, is broken, and it never healed. Perhaps it became infected. It's the sort of injury one might get in a bad fall. With his bad foot, Tut must have done a lot of falling.

Scientists have also found traces of malaria in the mummy. That's a serious, sometimes fatal, disease carried by mosquitoes. An infected leg combined with malaria probably killed the young pharaoh. At least that's the most popular theory today.[5]

No matter how he died, Tutankhamun will continue to be the most famous ancient Egyptian of them all.

CHAPTER 3

Mount Vesuvius the Killer

The ground was shaking again, but the people of Pompeii didn't pay much attention.

More than nineteen hundred years ago, their small city was a beautiful spot between Mount Vesuvius and the Mediterranean Sea. The climate was sunny and warm. Cool breezes from the sea kept it from getting too hot. Rich Romans built vacation homes there. Its shops, temples, and gymnasiums were busy places.

Pompeii had suffered a serious earthquake in 62 CE. Water pipes had broken and buildings had fallen. After that, the ground occasionally rumbled without causing serious damage. Some people kept plaster handy to repair little cracks that kept appearing in their walls.

The Romans had forgotten that Vesuvius was a volcano. They thought it was a pretty green mountain. They didn't know that earthquakes can be a sign a volcano is about to erupt.

Pompeii Is Destroyed

Then, on a summer morning in 79 CE, the earth shook and there was a horrible noise as the top blew off Vesuvius. Smoke and ash poured out of the broken mountain, darkening the sky. Fire was also exploding out of the giant hole. Pumice stones so hot that they were on fire shot into the air.

Terrified people tried to save themselves. One family hid in their cellar. There, they were safe from the ash and falling rocks. But poisonous gases had begun to leak out of Vesuvius and the cracks in the ground. The people in the cellar started to faint. One of them finally realized they needed fresh air. He grabbed his key and headed for the door, but he had moved too late. He collapsed before he could open it. All eighteen people in the cellar died.

A guard dog yanked at his chain, but he could not pull free. The poor animal choked to death as he was buried in ash.

A young girl thought the shower would soon end. If she could just keep the ash out of her nose and mouth for a few minutes, it would stop, and she would be safe. So she fell to the ground and pulled her dress up over her head, but the ash kept falling, and she was smothered.

This painting by Russian artist Karl Pavlovich Briullov (1799-1852), titled *The Last Day of Pompeii* and created in 1833, shows the people of Pompeii trying to escape the eruption of Vesuvius.

Pliny the Younger was a teenaged witness. He had been staying with his uncle, Pliny the Elder, a famous Roman author, philosopher, and military leader. "You could hear the shrieks of women, the wailing of infants, and the shouting of men; some were calling their parents, others their children or their wives . . ." he wrote. "People bewailed their own fate or that of their relatives, and there were some who prayed for death."[1]

For two days the ground shook, and Vesuvius rained death. "At last the darkness thinned," Pliny wrote. "We were terrified to see everything changed, buried deep in ashes like snowdrifts."[2] In places, the ash was 30 feet (9 meters) deep. Pompeii was gone.

Forgotten for Centuries

After a few years, grass and trees began growing over the city. People forgot it had ever even existed. Then, almost seventeen centuries later, in 1748, a farmer digging in a vineyard found a buried wall. Soon workers began uncovering the ancient doomed city. The work has continued now for nearly three centuries. Today, the ashes have been cleared away. Visitors can walk the ancient streets and look at the many walls and columns that weren't wrecked by the eruption.

An Italian archaeologist, Giuseppe Fiorelli (1823–1896), was the man who

Pliny the Elder

Pliny the Elder was a fleet commander in the Roman navy. When Vesuvius erupted, he took a small boat to rescue two of his friends. Pumice and cinders were falling, and his friends were frantic with worry. But after he landed, the winds changed and, for a while, the boat couldn't leave. To calm his friends, Pliny organized a feast. Then he took a long, leisurely bath. By then, the ground was shaking and buildings were beginning to fall. Pliny's friends tried to drag him away, but he couldn't get up. He had died, probably of a heart attack. His friends escaped without him on his boat.

These are the ruins of Pompeii as they appear today.

made it possible for us to feel the agony of Vesuvius's victims. In 1864, he discovered that the ash had hardened around their bodies. When the bodies decayed, they had left perfect molds surrounding their bones. Fiorelli poured plaster into the molds. When it hardened, he chipped away the ash. That left a white plaster mummy filled with bones, showing exactly how the victims had appeared when they died.

Hundreds of the mummies have been prepared by Fiorelli and more recent archaeologists. These plaster mummies aren't of as much interest to scientists as Ötzi the Iceman or King Tut. The skin and organs have totally decomposed, and the bones are stuck inside the plaster. The teeth are visible on those who died gasping or screaming for breath, but no other body parts can be inspected.

What is left is a horrifying moment frozen forever by ash and then plaster. Although the ash destroyed a lot of information on the bodies, archaeologists are still learning about how the people lived, what they ate, and even what their gardens looked like. And we have a very accurate picture of how these unfortunate people died.

Scientists have recently begun conducting CT scans of the plaster mummies. This has given them a clear view of the skeletons inside. They have discovered that many of the bodies suffered damage to their skulls, probably caused by falling buildings. Most of their teeth were in excellent shape. The people of Pompeii must have had a low-sugar, high-fiber diet.[3]

Even though they are made of plaster, the mummies of Pompeii seem more real because they look like real people. The terrified, twisted dog still seems to be struggling for his life nearly two thousand years after he died. We wish that the ash had not been as thick so that the little girl with the dress pulled over her head could have run to safety. Their mummies, and those of the people who died with them, help us to understand what it must have been like to have been in Pompeii that terrible day.

The victim's teeth are visible in this plaster mummy from Pompeii.

CHAPTER 4

Tollund Man, a Bog Body

On May 6, 1950, Grethe Hojgaard watched her husband Viggo and his brother Emil dig with spades near their home in Tolland Fen, Denmark. They were bringing up peat, a dark soil formed by layers of dead plants packed down in soggy ground. They would cut the peat into chunks, dry them and burn them as fuel.

The brothers were down about 7 feet (2 m) when their spades hit something hard. Grethe thought it looked like a head. The brothers wanted to keep digging, but she told them to stop. Then Grethe started digging with her hands until her fingers came under a cap on the head of a body.[1] Soon they were looking into a peaceful reddish-brown face. He seemed to be sleeping.

But there was a rope around his neck.

Peat has been cut from a bog and left out to dry.

A schoolboy from Copenhagen, Denmark's capital, was missing. Grethe's family wondered if the body was his. Perhaps he had been strangled, then dumped in the peat.

A Victim from Long Ago

The police arrived. The face didn't match the missing boy. In fact, nobody recognized him. The police decided he wasn't even the victim of a recent crime. The body was taken to Copenhagen's National Museum.

Since his name was unknown, the victim was called Tollund Man, after the modern town where he was found.

Professor Peter Glob (1911–1985) examined the rope around his neck. It was obvious Tollund man had died by hanging. The

Today, thousands of years after his death, Tollund Man still appears to be sleeping.

ends of the rope hung down his back. He was wearing only a belt and his cap. Not all of his body was as well preserved as the head, and some of his bones were showing, but his internal organs were in great shape.

Over the next several weeks, Glob began to unravel the mystery of Tollund Man. It was obvious he wasn't accustomed to tough physical work because his hands and feet were soft and his fingernails weren't broken. By examining the stomach and intestines, Glob determined that Tollund Man's last meal had been a porridge made out of grains and seeds.

The condition of Tollund Man's teeth led the professor to believe that he was at least twenty years old. There was stubble on his chin. His hair was short—about 2 inches (5 cm) long. And it was red—just like his skin.

Glob was able to report conclusively that a murder had been committed, but the "crime" had taken place almost two thousand years before. And in fact, Tollund Man himself had probably wanted to die.[2]

Don't Make Nerthus Mad

Scientists eventually used radiocarbon dating to determine Tollund Man had died around 400 BCE. Back then, Tollund Fen was already an area with many bogs. The people who lived there worshipped many gods and goddesses. One of the most powerful was Nerthus, the goddess of fertility, whose symbol was a twisted rope. If she was happy, the people would have a successful harvest. But if she was angry, the crops wouldn't grow and the people might starve.

The ancient farmers around Tollund figured they knew how to keep Nerthus happy. One of the men was picked each year to be her husband. That was why his hands were soft. He had been worshiped as a god, and he did not have to work. But at the end of a religious festival, he was sacrificed to his "wife," Nerthus, hanged by the twisted rope that was her symbol.[3]

The goddess Nerthus was worshipped by Tollund Man's people and others. This artwork depicts her being pulled by oxen on the German island of Rügen in the Baltic Sea.

There were no scratches or other evidence of a struggle on Tollund Man's body. He had wanted to die. It was his duty and an honor. After being strangled, he believed that he would be with the goddess forever, and his death would guarantee a fine harvest for his people, keeping them alive another year.[4]

The Mummy-Maker

After his death, Tollund Man's body was lowered into the sacred bog. His people had no way of knowing that burying him there would preserve his body for thousands of years. A bog is a soggy low area from which water cannot drain. Layers and layers of dead plants build up on the bottom under the water. Over the years, the plants are packed down and decay. They turn into peat, which looks like black dirt.

Moss grows over the soggy bog, trapping the water under the surface. That causes the water to lose its oxygen. The moss gives off acid that kills bacteria. Without oxygen and bacteria in the water, nothing in the bog can decay. It just turns red. The bog becomes a mummy-maker, and bodies in it can last forever.

Today, the head of Tollund Man is on display in Silkeborg, Denmark. Visitors can come face to face with a man who died 2,400 years ago. They can look at his calm, peaceful expression and wonder if they would have had the courage to face death as he did.

Protecting the Bogs

Don't expect to see many more new bog bodies. In modern times, peat is not used much for fuel. Other sources are cheaper and easier to find. There are also complaints that digging through the bogs damages the environment. When Tollund Man was found, villagers were using spades. It was easy to spot body parts. Today's digging is done by big machines that could easily destroy any bodies before they're noticed.

CHAPTER 5

Princess Kadyn the Ice Maiden

Ukok is flat and cold and far away from almost everybody. It has no trees. The word *Ukok* means "the end of everything." Today snow leopards think it's a great home.

Scientists call Ukok a plateau, or steppe. It sits on the Altai Mountains of Russian Siberia near the borders of China, Kazakhstan, and Mongolia.

Two thousand years ago, Ukok was the home of the Pazyryks. They were nomads, who moved from place to place, always looking for fresh pastures to feed their sheep. Each spring they stayed in a special spot they called the Pastures of Heaven. This, they believed, was the closest place on earth to heaven. It was a perfect spot to bury their dead.

One of the dead was a young woman whose body was covered with beautiful, elaborate tattoos. It had carefully been prepared for its journey. The skull had been opened and the brain removed. All the internal organs and muscles had been scraped away. The Pazyryks then stuffed the body with herbs, grasses, and wool, and sewed it back together.

This Pazyryk carpet showing deer and horsemen was found in a burial mound and dates back to the fifth or fourth century BCE.

The ground had thawed, so they could dig the pit and line it with logs. Chunks of mutton and horsemeat were left to provide nourishment on the way to the afterlife. Six horses dressed in beautiful harnesses were also buried with her. The body itself was laid on its side in a coffin made from a hallowed log.

A wooden lid was placed over the log walls, forming a small room around the coffin. Then the pit was refilled with dirt. On top was a kurgan—a mound of rocks. The Pazyryks then left the Pastures of Heaven.

Opening the Kurgan

In the summer of 1993, 2,500 years later, Natalia Polosmak (1956–), a Russian archaeologist, brought her students to the steppes of Siberia. She led her crew to a kurgan. Under the mound of rocks, she expected to find at least traces of a Pazyryk burial chamber. Since the kurgans were so visible, she knew that many of them had been looted by tribes that came later. This time she was lucky. When the rocks and dirt were cleared away, there was the unbroken lid of a chamber. No one had been inside for twenty-five centuries!

The archaeologist knew the most she could expect to find was a skeleton and a few artifacts. When the lid was removed, all she could see was ice. Sometime after the burial, the entire chamber had filled with water that was still frozen. Polosmak wondered when the water had entered the chamber. If it had leaked in soon after the burial and frozen quickly, everything inside would be very well preserved.

Melting the Ice

With the lid off, the sun warmed the chamber for the first time in centuries. Soon, the ice began turning into mush. To speed the melting, Polosmak filled huge drums with water from a nearby lake. After the water was heated by a blow torch, it was poured cup by cup onto the ice. Soon she could see a long wooden coffin, then two small tables holding mutton and horsemeat. Since the food hadn't completely rotted away, Polosmak knew it must have frozen very quickly after the burial. As the hot water hit the meat, it formed a kind of hot soup. Polosmak could smell the 2,500-year-old meal.

As the deeper ice turned to mush, she could see the rotting bodies of the six horses. Pieces of their brown coats still hung to their bones. Each of them had a hole in its skull made by the blow of the axe. Soon their thawed bodies began to stink in the sun.

Polosmak turned her attention to the coffin. When long bronze nails were pulled out, the lid could be removed. Inside was a solid block of dark ice. As she poured hot water from a cup onto the ice inside the coffin, the archaeologist began to see shapes emerge. The first thing she recognized was a jawbone. Then, a chunk of flesh on a cheek was revealed.

Soon, the whole mummy was free of ice, and Polosmak could see it was covered by a fur blanket. When she pulled back the blanket she could see the body wore a flowing woolen skirt and a silk tunic. It also had a long wooden headdress decorated by eight carved cats covered with gold. The mummy had been a noble woman. Reporters would call her the Ice Maiden, but the people who still lived in the Altai Mountains named her Princess Kadyn.

Much of the body was still covered by soft skin. "We pulled back carefully the clothing, and on her left arm, the right thumb, and then again on her left shoulder are these amazing tattoos," said Jeanne Smoot, one of Polosmak's students. "Creatures just in immediate action poses . . . They have amazing horns that end in flowers, fantastic creatures."[1]

Who Was Princess Kadyn?

Polosmak decided she must have been very important to her people. Why else would she have been given such a special burial? The Pazyryks could not have left six horses in the tombs of every dead member of the tribe. Even though she was still in her twenties, Princess Kadyn must have done something very special to deserve such treatment.

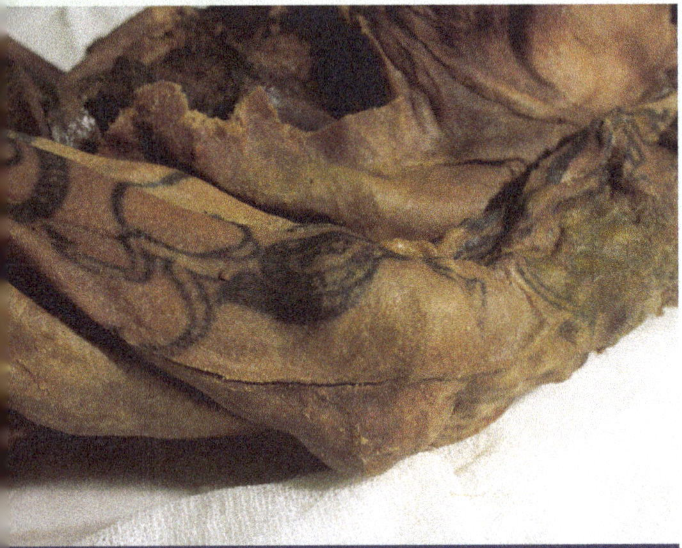

Even after thousands of years, an animal tattoo is still quite visible on the arm of Princess Kadyn.

The Ice Maiden was taken from Ukok to Moscow, Russia, where scientists investigated the mummy. MRI scans have revealed that she had probably died of cancer. She was also suffering from a bone infection. The scientists discovered several injuries. They decided she had probably been hurt in a fall from a horse.[2]

Natalia Polosmak's discovery pieced together more information about the history of the Pazyryks. She and other Russian scientists wished to do further digging in Ukok. But archaeologists are no longer allowed to dig in the Pastures of Heaven. The Altai people, who live there today, do not want it disturbed.

"People here have suffered much misfortune since the Ice Princess was disturbed," said one. He said it was a sacrilege to pour hot water on ancient remains.[3]

"The dead cannot be disturbed," said councilman Akay Kine, "and especially they cannot be held on public display and carried around the world. After she was dug out, we immediately saw earthquakes, floods, and hail which were not known previously."[4]

And so it was decided to bring her home. After nineteen years, Princess Kadyn's mummy was returned to the Altai Republic in 2012 to be reburied at the site of the original kurgan.[5]

Saving the Princess

Princess Kadyn's mummy barely made it out of Ukok. The helicopter carrying it crashed. Then the mummy was placed in a freezer. Unfortunately, the freezer had recently held cheese. Soon mold began to grow on the Ice Maiden. Embalming experts in Moscow volunteered to help. They are the ones who have preserved the body of Russian leader Vladimir Lenin (1870–1924) and keep it on display nearly a century after his death. They were finally able to save Princess Kadyn.

Chapter Notes

Chapter 1. Ötzi the Iceman

1. David Leveille, "Researchers May Have Cracked the Case of How Otzi the Iceman Died," PRI, April 6, 2017, https://www.pri.org/stories/2017-04-06/researchers-may-have-cracked-case-how-tzi-iceman-died.
2. Sandy Fritz, "Who Was the Iceman?" *Popular Science* 242, no. 2 (February 1993), p. 46.
3. David Roberts, "The Ice Man: Lone Visitor From the Copper Age," *National Geographic* 184, no. 6 (June 1993), p. 47.
4. "Otzi the Iceman: The Mummy," South Tyrol Museum of Archaeology, 2016, http://www.iceman.it/en/the-mummy/.
5. DW staff, "'Curse of the Iceman' Linked to Scientist's Death," DW.com, November 6, 2005, http://www.dw.com/en/curse-of-the-iceman-linked-to-scientists-death/a-1765550.
6. Leveille.
7. Bruce Bower, "Otzi the Iceman Froze to Death," Science News, April 21, 2017, https://www.sciencenews.org/article/otzi-iceman-froze-death.

Chapter 2. Tutankhamun the Boy King

1. Rishi Iyengar, "Tutankhamun Had a Clubfoot and His Parents Were Probably Siblings," Time.com, October 22, 2014, http://time.com/3530474/tutankhamun-clubfoot-parents-incest-genetics/.

2. Bob Brier, *The Murder of Tutankhamen: A True Story* (New York, N.Y.: Berkley Books, 1998), p.?
3. Jennie Cohen, "Did a Hippo Kill King Tut?" History.com, November 2, 2010, https://www.history.com/news/did-a-hippo-kill-king-tut.
4. "What killed Tutankhamun?" History Extra, August 25, 2014, https://www.historyextra.com/period/ancient-egypt/what-killed-tutankhamun/.
5. Ker Than, "King Tut Mysteries Solved: Was Disabled, Malarial, and Inbred," *National Geographic News,* February 17, 2010, https://news.nationalgeographic.com/news/2010/02/100216-king-tut-malaria-bones-inbred-tutankhamun/.

Chapter 3. Mount Vesuvius the Killer

1. "The Destruction of Pompeii, 79 AD," Eyewitness to History, 1999, http://www.eyewitnesstohistory.com/pompeii.htm.
2. Betty Radice, trans.,"Pliny the Younger, Letters 6.16 and 6.20," Arizona.edu, http://www.u.arizona.edu/~afutrell/film%20anc%20world/pliny%20vesuvius.htm (accessed May 8, 2018).
3. Victoria Woollaston, "Revealed—What's Inside the Pompeii Mummies: Incredible CT Scans Show Bodies in Unprecedented Detail Laying Bare Their Bones, Delicate Facial Features and Even Perfect Teeth," DailyMail, September 29, 2015, http://www.dailymail.co.uk/sciencetech/article-3253660/Peering-inside-Pompeii-s-tragic-victims-Incredible-CT-scans-reveal-bodies-unprecedented-laying-bare-bones-delicate-facial-features-dental-cavities.html.

Chapter 4. Tollund Man, a Bog Body

1. “Account of an Eyewitness,” The Tollund Man—A Face from Prehistoric Denmark, 2004 http://www.tollundman.dk/et-lig-dukker-op.asp.
2. P. V. Glob, “Lifelike Man Preserved 2,000 Years in Peat,” *National Geographic* 105, no. 3 (March 1954), p. 419.
3. Maurice Shadbolt, “Who Killed the Bog Men of Denmark? And Why?” *Reader’s Digest* 110, no. 662 (June 1977), p. 204.
4. Glob, p. 428.

Chapter 5. Princess Kadyn the Ice Maiden

1. “Ice Mummies: Siberian Ice Maiden,” NOVA, PBS.org, November 24, 1998, http://www.pbs.org/wgbh/nova/transcripts/2517siberian.html.
2. Dominique Mosbergen “Now We Know What Killed the Ancient ‘Ice Princess,’ and Why She Had That Marijuana,” *Huffington Post,* December 6, 2017, https://www.huffingtonpost.com/2014/10/16/siberian-ice-princess-cancer-cannabis_n_5993052.html.
3. “Siberian Princess Reveals Her 2,500 Year Old Tattoos,” *Siberian Times,* August 14, 2012, http://siberiantimes.com/culture/others/features/siberian-princess-reveals-her-2500-year-old-tattoos/.
4. Will Stewart, “Siberia’s Tattooed Princess Revealed: 2,500-year-old Mummy to Go on Public Display, but Will Be Draped to Hide Her Modesty,” Daily Mail, June 3, 2016, http://www.dailymail.co.uk/sciencetech/article-3623874/Siberia-s-tattooed-princess-revealed-2-500-year-old-mummy-public-display-draped-fur-hide-modesty.html.
5. Adam Gauntlett, “Siberian Elders Vote to Bury Ice Mummy to Ward Off Earthquakes, Floods,” *Escapist Magazine,* August 20, 2014, http://www.escapistmagazine.com/news/view/136946-Russia-Today-Siberian-Ice-Maiden-to-be-Reburied-thanks-to-Activist-Campaign#&gid=gallery_3027&pid=1

Glossary

Amun One of the most important gods of ancient Egypt.

archaeologist A scientist who studies past human cultures and civilizations.

Aten The ancient Egyptian god of the sun.

bacteria Tiny one-celled microorganisms which cause decomposition.

bog Wet, spongy ground that usually forms when decaying plant growth fills in a swamp.

chariot An ancient two-wheeled vehicle pulled by horses.

CT scan A series of detailed pictures of areas inside a body taken by a computer linked to an X-ray machine.

curator The manager of museum displays.

embalm To preserve a human body.

formaldehyde A chemical used to preserve the bodies of the dead.

hieroglyphics A form of writing that uses pictures to symbolize words and sounds.

malaria A disease spread by mosquitoes that can cause death.

MRI scan A picture of the body produced by magnetic resonance imaging.

plateau High, level ground.

Valley of the Kings An Egyptian valley where many pharaohs were buried.

Further Reading

Books

Aldhouse-Green, Miranda. *Bog Bodies Uncovered: Solving Europe's Ancient Mystery.* London, UK: Thames and Hudson, 2015.

Bower, Tamara. *The Mummy Makers of Egypt.* New York, NY: Seven Stories Press, 2016.

Farndon, John, and Maurizio Campidelli. *How to Live Like an Egyptian Mummy Maker.* London, England: Hungry Tomato, 2016.

Lanser, Amanda. Ötzi *the Iceman.* Minneapolis, MN: Essential Library, 2015.

Levy, Janey, *The City of Pompeii.* New York, NY: Gareth Stevens, 2015.

Websites

Silkeborg Public Library

www.tollundman.dk/

Explore the life, discovery, and preservation of Tollund Man.

South Tyrol Museum of Archaeology

www.iceman.it/en/the-mummy/

View pictures and learn more facts about Ötzi the Iceman.

UShistory.org

www.ushistory.org/civ/3d.asp

Read a step-by-step description of mummification.

Index